THE
BIG
BOOK OF
NATURE
ART

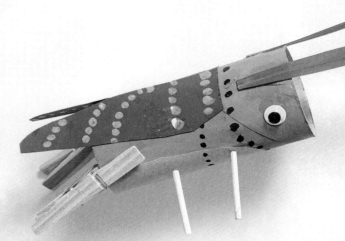

Words and pictures
YUVAL ZOMMER

Can you find . . .

. . . exactly the same ant
15 times in this book?

THE
BIG
BOOK OF
NATURE
ART

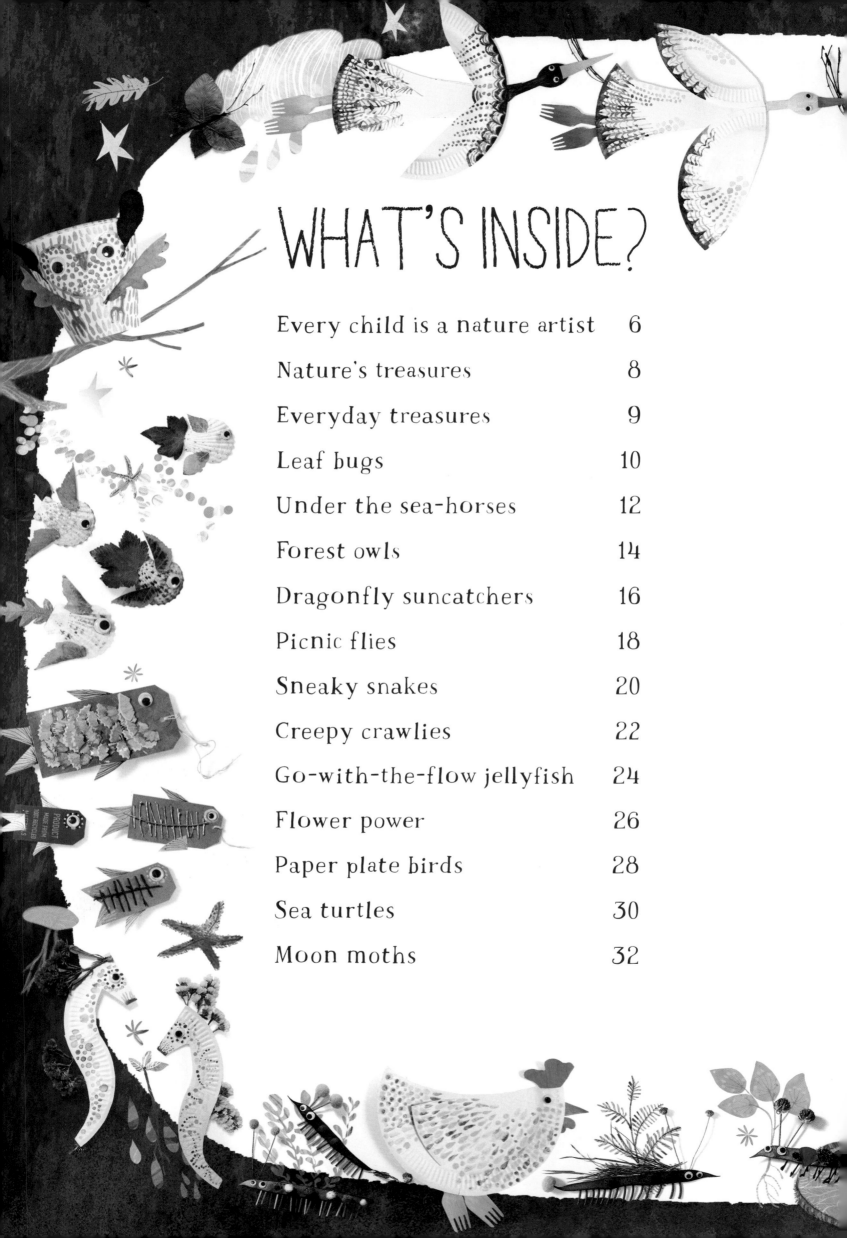

WHAT'S INSIDE?

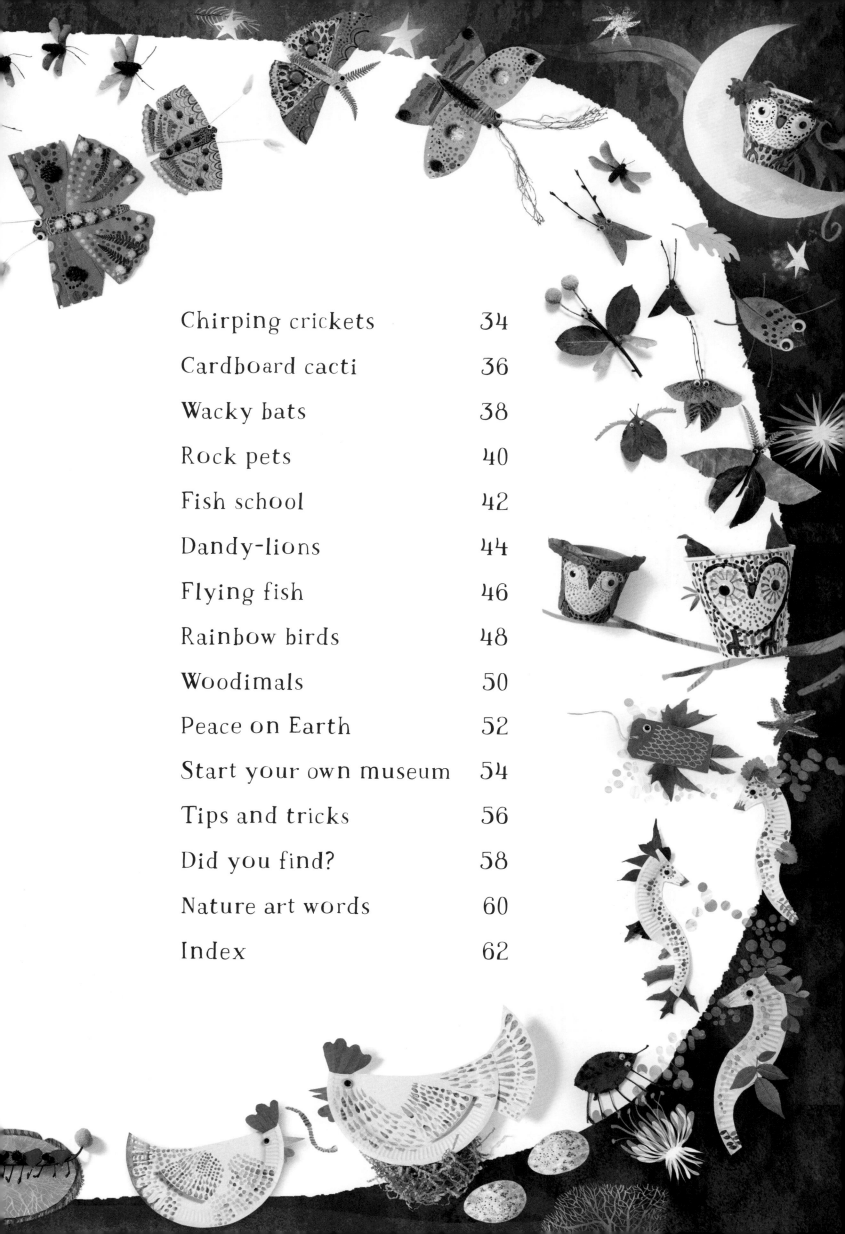

EVERY CHILD IS
A NATURE ARTIST

Have you ever marveled at a bird's feather or felt compelled to collect pebbles? Or perhaps you've drawn circles in the sand or made a sculpture out of stones?

Since early humans made the first handprints onto cave walls, we have found ways to express ourselves—it's in our nature. What's more, nature itself feeds us creative inspiration all year long—from spring's colorful blossoms to the sparkle of stars in a dark winter sky.

As Pablo Picasso said, "Every child is an artist." I hope this book will help you discover how easy it is to make art that is inspired by and made from nature. Every child is a nature artist!

Because we all belong to nature and nature belongs to us all . . .

YUVAL ZOMMER

Before you start . . .

1. Four steps are all you need
Every activity in this book has been carefully tried
and tested, and can be achieved in just four steps.

2. Break the rules
We value artists so much because they are original. I always
encourage young artists to be original too. Look at the instructions
as a starting point, and then have fun breaking the rules!

3. Let your children choose
Look for ways to help your child assert their independence by
making choices—it might be what color paint they use, which
leaf they decorate, or which activity you embark on.

4. Enjoy the process
Above all else, make sure you have fun! The purpose of these
projects is not to produce the most amazing moon moth but
to connect with nature and let your creativity run wild!

NATURE'S TREASURES

The pleasure of nature art starts before the making even begins.

To start, discover the joy of foraging. Nature's treasures are everywhere—in your garden, at your local park, at the beach, in the forest, and even in the city! There is a world of amazing materials right under your nose.

Maybe you'll spot a twig that looks like a monkey's arm, a shoe-shaped rock, or a leaf that reminds you of a face. It's all about what natural treasures mean to you. Once you start foraging, you might not be able to stop.

EVERYDAY TREASURES

But foraging doesn't just apply to nature. **The Big Book of Nature Art** is about foraging closer to home, too—putting to use the everyday treasures that are all around us.

Whether it's reusing wool from an old sweater, recycling cereal boxes, or repurposing paper towel tubes, every item holds a world of possibility.

And when you bring nature's treasures and everyday treasures together . . . well, that's when things get really exciting.

It's time to reconnect with the treasures all around us—**it's time to create nature art.**

LEAF BUGS

You'll need: sticks, pine cones, dry leaves (matching pairs), helicopter seeds, small twigs, glue, googly eyes

1. Choose a selection of sticks and pine cones. These are your bugs' bodies.

stick body

seed wings

2. Take a pair of matching leaves. Glue them to each side of your bug's body to make wings. Some bugs could have two sets of wings.

3. Next, you can add tiny twigs for the antennae or legs, and googly eyes.

twig legs

googly
eyes

leaf
wings

twig
antennae

4. Finally, arrange
all your bugs on a piece
of paper. Draw their natural
habitat. Remember, to a bug a flower
is as tall as a tree and a rock is as
high as a mountain!

Did you know? Bugs don't have skeletons
inside their bodies like humans do. They
have an exoskeleton, or "outside skeleton"
—a shell that protects them.

UNDER THE SEA-HORSES

You'll need: paper plates, leaves or seaweed or flowers, paints, scissors, glue, googly eyes

1. Cut your paper plate into a seahorse shape—kind of like a tall "S" with a long head.

leafy crown

paper plate

2. Add paint splotches to create a beautiful pattern on the seahorse's tummy and face. Stick on a googly eye.

coronet

3. Stick flowers, leaves, or seaweed onto your seahorse to give it a "coronet"—that's the crown on its head. You can also add fins to the body.

leafy fin

4. Draw a floaty seaweed forest for your seahorse to swim in and cling on to when the ocean currents get rough!

Did you know? Seahorses might look cute but they're talented hunters. They sneak up on tiny fish and suck them up their snouts like a vacuum cleaner!

flower fin

FOREST OWLS

You'll need: paper cups, leaves, paints (or crayons), glue, googly eyes

1. Take a paper cup and flatten it slightly by pinching the rim inwards at each edge.

paper cup

leafy tufts

2. Use paints or crayons to draw a face on your owl. Add a beak and feet, and stick on some googly eyes. Now paint a feathery pattern all over your owl's body.

googly eyes

leaf wings

3. Stick two large leaves to the top of the owl's face to make tufts. You can also stick leaves on the sides as wings.

14

4. Owls like to come out when it's dark, so remember to close the curtains before taking your owl on a flying tour of your home!

Did you know?
Owls can turn their heads almost all the way around —making it much easier to spot tasty mice to munch on.

DRAGONFLY SUNCATCHERS

You'll need: black cardboard, acetate sheets or recycled cellophane, metallic pens, scissors or a craft knife, glue, googly eyes

1. Ask an adult for help cutting out a dragonfly shape from cardboard. It should have a really long body with two big wings coming out of the top.

black cardboard

2. Ask an adult for help hollowing out sections of the wings to make a pattern. Next, use pens to add metallic sparkles.

3. Stick pieces of colorful acetate or recycled cellophane to the panels in the wings. Add a googly eye.

acetate

googly eye

shadow wings

4. Take your dragonfly outside. Stand in strong sunlight, and take a look at its shadow. The second half of your dragonfly has magically appeared! Why not see how far it can fly?

Did you know? Dragonflies can see more colors than any other animal in the world!

PICNIC FLIES

You'll need: cardboard fruit packaging, notecards, clear packaging plastic, black cardstock, wooden beads, paints, scissors, glue, googly eyes

1. Cut out your fly's body from the cardboard fruit packaging. Paint it black and blue.

notecard wings

2. Cut out two wings from notecards or from plastic. Decorate the wings with paints. When they are dry, glue them to the body.

black card legs

cardboard fruit packaging

3. Cut out six legs and a pointy proboscis (a fly's long nose) from black card. Glue them to the body. Stick on two wooden beads and add googly eyes.

googly eyes

wooden beads

4. Ask a family member or friend to play the "spider" and close their eyes while you find a hiding place for your fly. When the spider opens their eyes, the hunt for the fly begins! Make a buzzing noise when they get close.

plastic wings

Did you know? Instead of using their tongues to taste food, flies use their feet. Yuck!

19

SNEAKY SNAKES

You'll need: cardboard, leaves or lentils or pine cones, sunflower seeds, scissors, paints, glue

1. Cut a long, squiggly snake out of cardboard. Remember to give it a head and wiggly body. Cut a long, forked tongue from the leftover cardboard.

2. Paint your snake a sneaky camouflage color and the tongue green or orange. Paint two sunflower seeds red or yellow for the eyes. Once the eyes and tongue are dry, glue them to your snake's head.

sunflower seed eyes

forked tongue

cardboard body

3. Glue lentils or pine cones or leaves onto the cardboard body to give your snake a splendid scaly pattern.

leaves

lentils

pine cones

4. Can you slither across the room on your tummy? I bet your snake can . . .

Did you know? When a snake sticks its tongue out, it's not just to hissss. Snakes have bad eyesight, so they use their tongues to find their way around!

21

CREEPY CRAWLIES

You'll need: long seed pods (like carob or pea pods or runner beans), wool yarn or twigs, matchsticks, flower petals, pom poms, scissors, glue, googly eyes

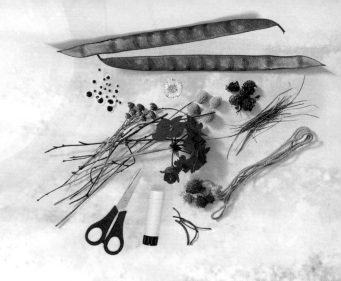

flower antennae

1. Choose a seed pod—this is your centipede's body. Chop up wool yarn into short pieces to make legs. Glue the legs to the back of the seed pod.

2. Choose which end of your long seed pod is the head. Add flower antennae or matchsticks topped with pom poms.

string legs

grass back

3. Add googly eyes for extra impact and decorate your centipede's body with petals or pom poms.

4. On a large piece of cardboard draw a maze or an underground warren for your centipedes to creep and crawl in!

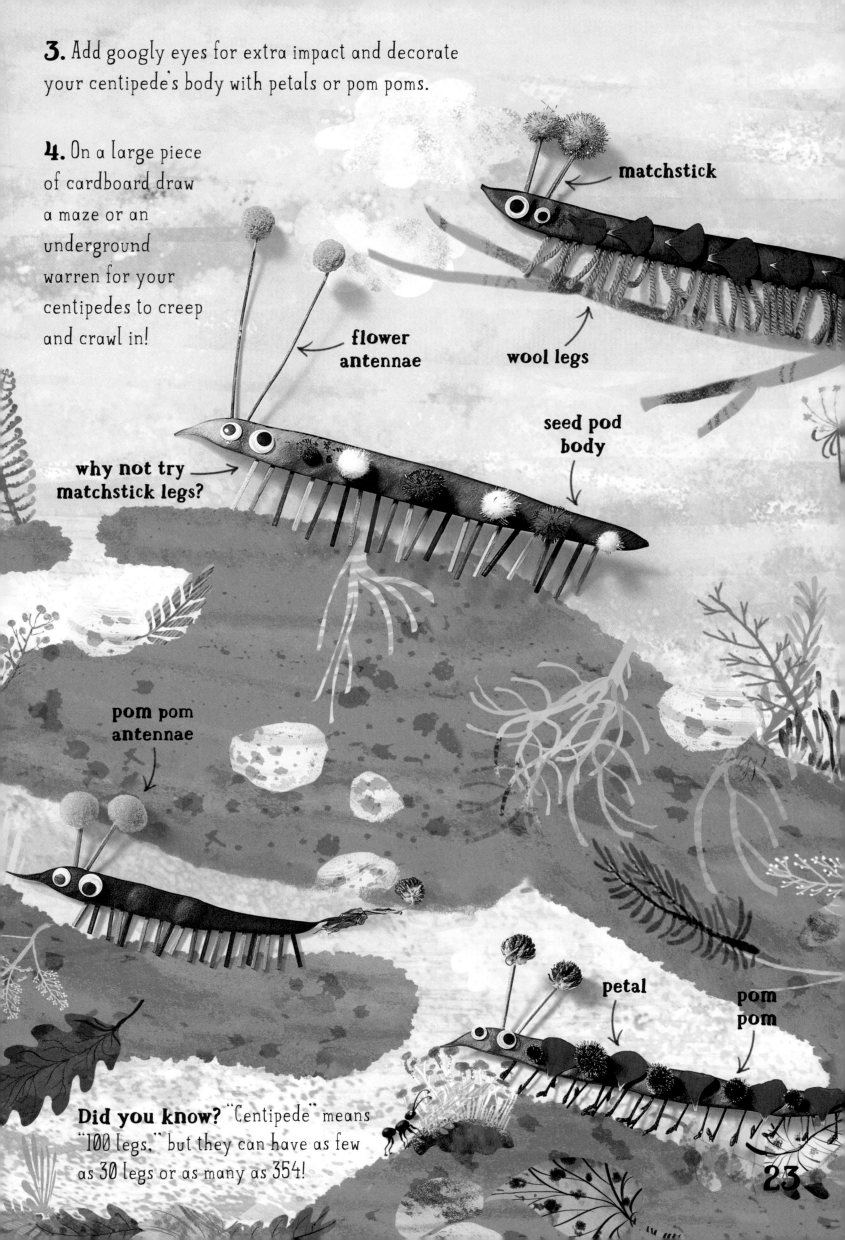

matchstick

flower antennae

wool legs

seed pod body

why not try matchstick legs?

pom pom antennae

petal

pom pom

Did you know? "Centipede" means "100 legs," but they can have as few as 30 legs or as many as 354!

23

GO-WITH-THE-FLOW JELLYFISH

You'll need: bubble wrap, string or yarn, scissors, glue or tape, markers, googly eyes

bubble wrap body

yarn tentacles

1. Cut out two matching capital Ds from bubble wrap—these will make your jellyfish's body. Stick them together along the curved edges. Leave the straight edge unstuck.

2. Cut long pieces of string or yarn and bubble wrap to make your jellyfish's tentacles. Stick them to the straight edge of the body.

googly eyes

3. Use colored markers to decorate your jellyfish. Once the ink is dry, add googly eyes.

bubble wrap tentacles

4. Stick your hand inside your jellyfish to bring it to life. Let it swim through the air like it's under the sea.

Did you know? Jellyfish existed hundreds of millions of years before the first dinosaurs.

FLOWER POWER

You'll need: paper plates, pine cones or seeds or lentils or beans or dried flowers, pipe cleaners, wool yarn, card, paints, scissors, glue

1. Cut a paper plate into a bloom shape, with a circle at the center and lots of petals sticking out. Glue pine cones, lentils, beans, dried flowers, or seeds to the center.

pine cone

dried flowers

paper plate

lentils

wool roots

2. Paint your bloom in beautiful bright colors. Cut out card leaves and draw on leaf veins. Twist together green pipe cleaners to make a stem.

3. Stick the leaves to the stem. Next, cut pieces of yarn to make roots, and stick them to the bottom of the stem. Finally, stick your bloom to the top of the stem!

4. Once you've made a few flowers, you're ready to plant your garden! What creepy crawlies might live beneath the soil? Draw as many as you can imagine.

sunflower seeds

black beans

pipe cleaner stems

card

Did you know? Plants can use their roots to send each other messages like "Be careful, a swarm of hungry insects is coming!"

27

PAPER PLATE BIRDS

You'll need: paper plates, wooden spoons and forks, paints, scissors, glue, googly eyes

spoon

1. For the stork: take a paper plate and cut out two wings and a tail. Use a spoon for the head and two forks for the legs.

paper plate

forks

2. For the hen: take a paper plate and cut out a plump body. Cut up the remaining piece of plate to make a wing, a beak, a comb, and "wattles"—the red parts below a hen's beak. Use two forks for the legs.

paper plate

wing

beak

comb

wattles

3. For both the stork and the hen: paint feather patterns on the wings and tail. Paint the beak, comb and wattles red, and the legs yellow or orange. When all the body parts are dry, glue them together and add googly eyes.

googly eyes

4. Now it's time to go foraging! Find some sticks or shredded paper to make a cozy nest for your birds. If you're patient, they might have chicks before too long . . .

Did you know? A mother hen starts to teach different sounds and calls to her chicks before they even hatch from their eggs. Now that's getting a head start!

shredded paper

SEA TURTLES

You'll need: half of a coconut shell (or an old bowl), cardboard, white marker pen, paints, scissors, glue or tape, googly eyes

1. Use a white marker to draw a beautiful pattern on your turtle's shell.

coconut
shell

2. Cut out two big cardboard front flippers, two small back flippers, and a head. Paint them with green splotches.

3. Go over the green splotches with a white marker to make your turtle's skin look leathery. Stick the flippers and head to the coconut shell. Add googly eyes.

cardboard flippers

googly eyes

cardboard head

4. Imagine your turtle is your guide on an underwater adventure. What might you find if you put on your goggles and went exploring together?

Did you know? Most sea turtles spend their entire lives at sea, returning to the beach only to lay eggs. That's a long swim!

cardboard flippers

31

MOON MOTHS

You'll need: cardboard packaging, ferns or leaves, grass bristles, pom poms, paints, scissors, glue, googly eyes

1. Cut out a body and two sets of matching wings from cardboard packaging. Glue the wings onto the body to make your moth. Use paint to add beautiful patterns.

cardboard wings

cardboard body

fern

2. Keep decorating your moth by sticking on pom poms and small ferns or leaves.

pom pom

3. Next glue two grass bristles to your moth's head to make the antennae. Finish it off with some friendly googly eyes.

grass antennae

grass antennae

googly eyes

fern

twig antennae

4. Create a big crescent moon to help your moths find their way through the dark night. Now it's time to let them fly.

Did you know? Moths are amazing at hiding. Some of them look like bark, some look like other animals—and some look like bird poop!

CHIRPING CRICKETS

You'll need: cardboard tubes, grass, skewers (or matchsticks), clothespins, green paper or cardstock, paints, scissors, glue, googly eyes

1. Paint a cardboard tube green—this is your cricket's body.

2. Cut out two wings from green paper or cardstock. Decorate them with dots of paint. When they are dry, glue the wings to the top of your cricket's body.

3. Ask an adult to help you break a skewer into four pieces and poke the pieces through the cardboard tube to make legs. Clip two clothespins onto the back end of the tube as the cricket's springing legs.

cardboard
tube

clothespin
legs

skewer legs

blades of long green grass

4. Next, glue two long blades of green grass to the top of the cardboard tube for antennae. Finally, add googly eyes. Now you can take your cricket out to jump around in the long grass. How loud can you make it chirp and sing?

Did you know? A cricket's ears are located on its legs!

cardstock wings

35

CARDBOARD CACTI

You'll need: cardboard, plastic or paper cups, pom poms or matchsticks, lentils or rice or sand, scissors, paints, glue

1. Draw shapes on cardboard to make your cactus's body and many arms. Carefully cut them out.

matchsticks

cardboard

ice cream cup

2. Paint the cardboard green and add white dots in vertical lines. Stick the body and arms together to make a knobby cactus.

rice

pom poms

3. To make your cactus spiky or hairy or fuzzy, stick on pom poms or matchsticks. Now add your cactus to a cup filled with rice, lentils, or sand.

4. Why not make a desert of cacti in all shapes and sizes, and head off on a desert adventure?

plastic cup

paper cup

sand

lentils

Did you know? Some cacti grow their spikes, or "spines," in clusters. These work like little umbrellas to shade the cacti from the hot sun!

WACKY BATS

You'll need: cardboard cereal box, bark, leaves, twigs, sticks, scissors, glue, googly eyes

1. Draw a bat on a cereal box—remember their spiky ears and big wings. Carefully cut it out.

leaf wings

googly eyes

bark

2. Glue bark all over the bat's body, and add leaves on its wings and ears.

3. Add googly eyes. Now stick two twig legs to the bottom of the bat's body.

twig legs

4. Let your bat fly around, or flip it upside down if it would rather hang from a stick. Now you and your spooky bat can dim the lights and tell some scary stories.

leaf ears

Did you know? Bats are pollinators, just like bees. They help spread the seeds for bananas, nuts, and cacao—the main ingredient in chocolate!

ROCK PETS

You'll need: pebbles in all sorts of colors and sizes, leaves, twigs, ferns, pine needles—no glue or paint whatsoever!

1. Lay out your pebbles. Take time to notice their shapes, colors, and textures.

fern antlers

pebbles

2. Arrange your pebbles to create different animals. Or why not make a whole rock pet family?

twig horns

bushy grass tail

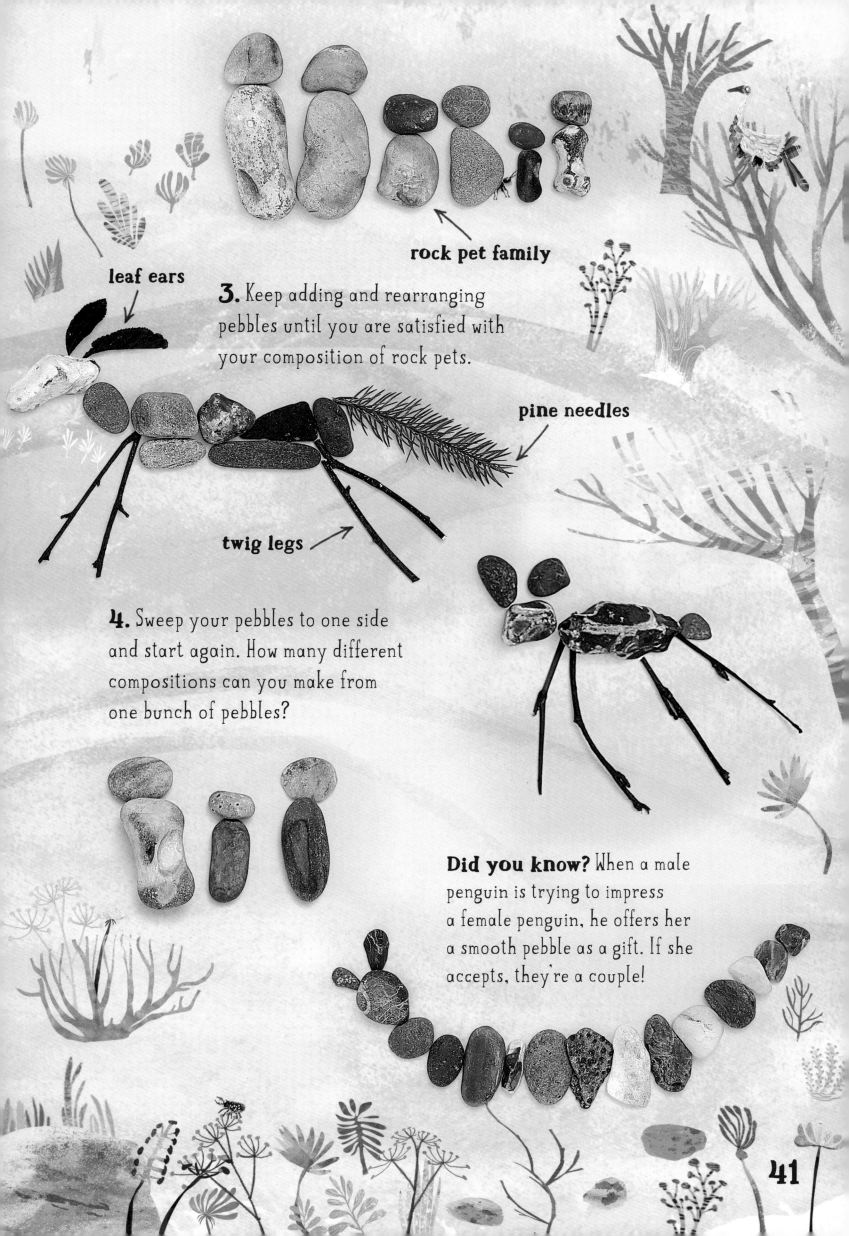

rock pet family

leaf ears

3. Keep adding and rearranging pebbles until you are satisfied with your composition of rock pets.

pine needles

twig legs

4. Sweep your pebbles to one side and start again. How many different compositions can you make from one bunch of pebbles?

Did you know? When a male penguin is trying to impress a female penguin, he offers her a smooth pebble as a gift. If she accepts, they're a couple!

FISH SCHOOL

You'll need: card labels (or seashells), lots of pencil shavings (use a pencil sharpener), leaves, scissors, glue, googly eyes

1. Take a card label and snip off the top two corners. This end of the label is your fish's head.

card label

leaf fins

leaf tail

2. Next, glue on some leaves to add two fins and a tail.

3. Add glue to your fish's body and stick on the pencil shavings to make scales. Now add an eye so that your fish can see you too.

pencil shaving scales

try using shells instead

4. Repeat until you have a whole shoal (or crowd) of fish. What are they swimming away from? Maybe it's a bigger fish or a shark—draw the mystery creature to complete the scene.

Did you know? Fish make noises to talk to one another, but they don't use their mouths like humans —they make sounds by vibrating their muscles.

DANDY-LIONS

You'll need: paper cups, cardboard, yellow petals, black beans, scissors, paints, glue

1. On a piece of cardboard draw a lion's front legs, back legs, a thin tail, a big circular mane, a head, and whiskers. Carefully cut them out.

cardboard

2. Paint the paper cup, legs, tail, and head yellow. Add features to the face and stick on black beans for eyes.

try making a lion sun using golden wheat and cardboard

3. Stick all of the other body parts to your paper cup.

petal tail

petal mane

black bean eyes

paper cup

4. Add glue to the mane and the tip of the tail, and stick on petals from yellow blooms. It's time to let your lions roar! Who's the loudest, you or your lion friend?

Did you know? The longer, darker, and thicker a lion's mane is, the more powerful and healthy he is likely to be.

45

FLYING FISH

You'll need: cardboard tube, crepe paper (in two colors), raffia, thread, stick, paints, googly eyes, scissors, glue

1. Paint scales on the cardboard tube—this is the fish's body. Let it dry, then add googly eyes.

2. Cut out four big, winglike fins from crepe paper. Cut out several smaller tail fins from raffia. Glue all of the fins to your flying fish's body.

raffia
tail fin

googly
eyes

crepe paper wings

cardboard
tube body

46

3. Ask an adult to punch a hole between the fish's eyes. Loop the thread through the hole, and tie the thread to your stick.

thread

4. Now take your fish outside and see how they "fly" in the wind!

Did you know? A flying fish swims in a school of up to one million others!

stick

47

RAINBOW BIRDS

You'll need: leaves (large and small), twigs, cardboard, notecard, paints, glue, scissors, tape, googly eyes

painted leaf

notecard

cardboard

1. Paint a large leaf in beautiful patterns to make tail feathers. Once this is dry, glue smaller leaves on top to add more feathers.

2. Cut out the bird's body and beak from cardboard. Paint the beak red. Cut out the bird's wing from notecards. Snip along the edges to make it feathery.

googly eyes

3. Glue the beak, wing, and tail feathers onto the body. Take two twigs and tape them to the bottom of the bird's body to make legs. Add a googly eye to bring your bird to life!

twigs

4. Repeat as many times as you like to make a flock. Now draw a tree where your birds can show off!

leaves

Did you know? The color white means danger to most birds, and they avoid it whenever they can. No wonder these birds are so colorful!

49

WOODIMALS

You'll need: wooden everyday items (like clothespins, wooden silverware, or pencils), shells, dried seaweed, paper or cardstock, paints, glue, googly eyes

1. Take an old spatula, wooden silverware, a clothespin, or an old pencil and use your imagination to uncover what creature lurks inside. Is it a whale or a shark or a sardine?

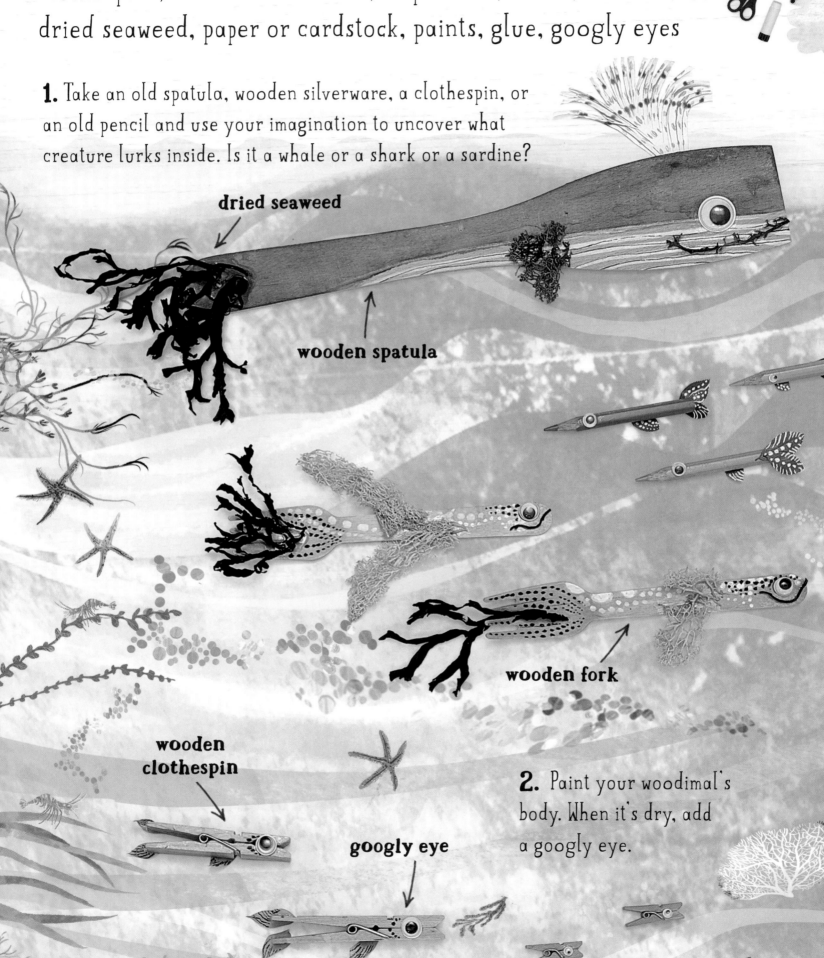

dried seaweed

wooden spatula

wooden fork

wooden clothespin

googly eye

2. Paint your woodimal's body. When it's dry, add a googly eye.

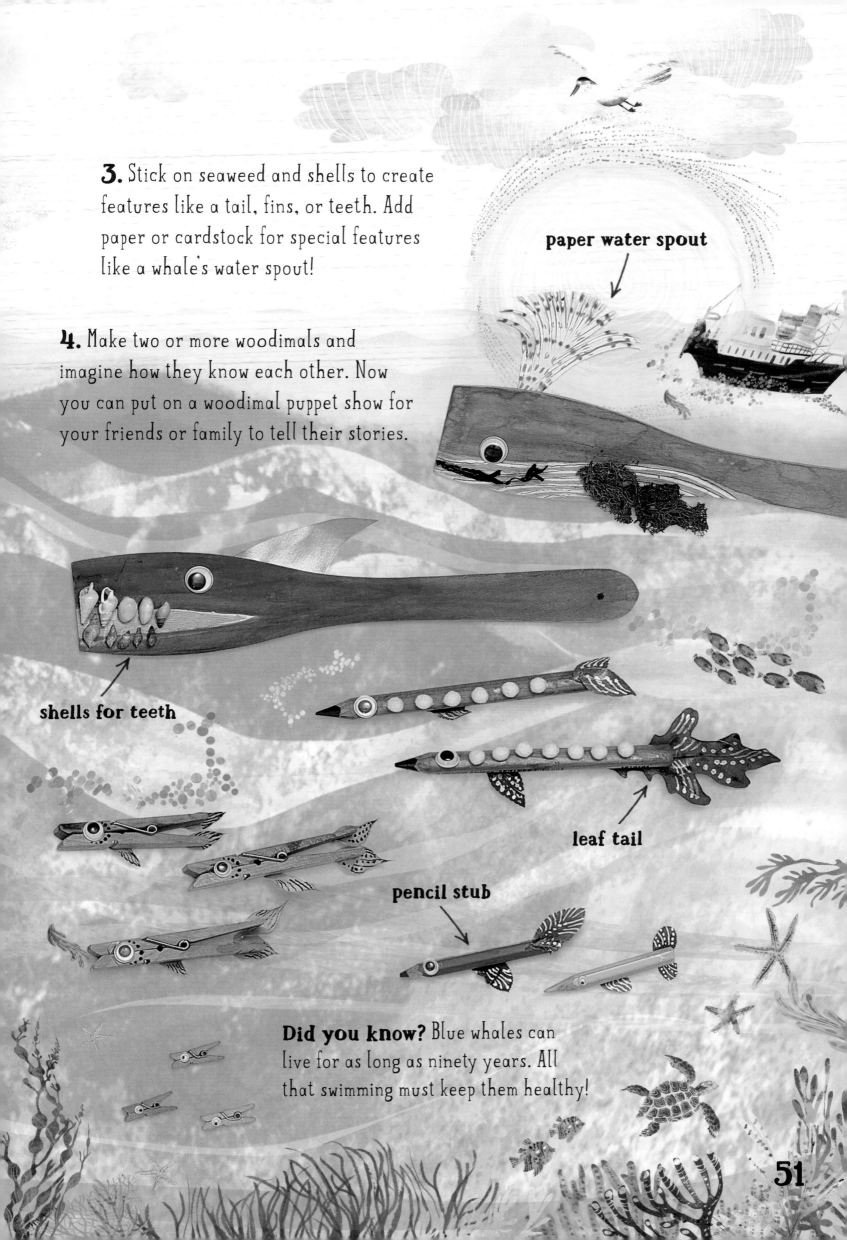

3. Stick on seaweed and shells to create features like a tail, fins, or teeth. Add paper or cardstock for special features like a whale's water spout!

4. Make two or more woodimals and imagine how they know each other. Now you can put on a woodimal puppet show for your friends or family to tell their stories.

paper water spout

shells for teeth

leaf tail

pencil stub

Did you know? Blue whales can live for as long as ninety years. All that swimming must keep them healthy!

51

PEACE ON EARTH

You'll need: cardboard (a pizza box or bigger), sand, natural materials (like flowers, pine cones, grass, moss, leaves or shells), cotton balls or small pebbles, scissors, blue paint, glue

1. Cut out a huge circle from cardboard—this is the world! Draw on the continents and paint the ocean blue.

2. Cover the continents with glue and sand where the land is.

sand

cardboard

try making a peaceful
dove out of cardboard

pebbles

moss

hand-shaped
paper wings

leaves

3. Next, add your natural
materials. You could add grass,
leaves, and moss where there is lots
of rain; flowers where the weather
is tropical; and cotton balls or
pebbles in the Arctic and Antarctic.

blooms

4. Have you made any
other crafted creatures
using this book? If so,
why not add them to your
beautiful planet? Try to
place them in the areas
where they might live
in real life.

Did you know? Earth is the only planet in our
solar system with liquid water on the surface. Think
of that next time you're drinking a glass of water!

shells

53

START YOUR OWN MUSEUM

Create your own collection
Now that you've had fun making nature art of your very own, it's time to share it with the world! Frame your creations and display them proudly in an exhibition.

Name: ....
Discovered: ....

Name: ....
Discovered: ....

Let your label do the talking
Create paper labels for each of your exhibits. Include the name of your species and where in the world it was discovered.

Name: Grassfoot
Discovered: At the park

Name: Twiggy
Discovered: In the forest

Name:
Discovered:

Name the explorer
Credit the explorer who first discovered your nature art creature in the wild. Was it Admiral Andy? Captain Cora? Or Sailor Sarah?

Name: Mothita
Discovered: On the porch

Name:
Discovered:

Name: Yuval
Discovered: @yuvalzommer

TIPS AND TRICKS

Make the most of nature's tools

You can use whatever materials you like to create the nature art projects in this book, but sometimes the best tools are the ones nature itself provides.

A brush with nature

Make your own natural paintbrushes by tying flowers, herbs, grasses, or leaves to the ends of sticks or twigs. Dip them in paint and see what different textures you can create.

Tools at your fingertips

Don't forget the natural tools you have at the end of your arms—your fingers! Dip your fingers in paint and enjoy the feeling of making patterns directly onto the page. Fingerprints can become everything from bees to centipedes to a field of beautiful blooms.

Handfuls of inspiration

Trace your hand on a piece of paper and cut out the shape. Your hands make fantastic feathers and wings. Dip your full hand in paint and make colorful handprints. Are they flamingos, flowers, or a fluttering butterfly? You decide!

DID YOU FIND

... the 15 hiding places of the ant from the beginning of the book?

Why not make your own ant? Stick three black beans to a piece of paper and draw on legs and antennae.

10–11 Leaf bugs

14–15 Forest owls

16–17 Dragonfly suncatchers

18–19 Picnic flies

20–21 Sneaky snakes

22–23 Creepy crawlies

26–27 Flower power

28-29 Paper plate birds

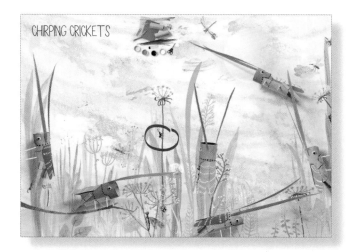

34-35 Chirping crickets

36-37 Cardboard cacti

38-39 Wacky bats

40-41 Rock pets

44-45 Dandy-lions

48-49 Rainbow birds

52-53 Peace on Earth

NATURE ART WORDS

How to talk like a nature art expert

Here are some words to use when you talk about nature art.

Creative collecting

Natural materials can be found by **foraging**. Always forage with an adult who can help you avoid plants that might be dangerous. Only pick leaves or petals that have fallen or are about to fall. Don't collect live animals—they prefer living in their natural home, or **habitat**.

Nature art isn't forever

Everything in nature is made from **organic matter**. This means your nature art will eventually rot, or **decompose**. This is nature's way of **recycling**!

Finding a new use for objects

Perhaps you have some old pencils at home, or an unraveling wooly sweater? Find a way to **repurpose** these objects and give them a new life.

Choose to be nature's friend

Choose to be more **environmentally friendly.** Use **recycled** materials and **reuse** things instead of throwing them away. Share your art supplies and tools with your friends.

INDEX

To my mother with all my love

With special thanks to Kate Haynes
for all the support and enthusiasm

The Big Book of Nature Art © 2023 Yuval Zommer
Photography © 2023 Thames & Hudson Ltd, London

Words and pictures by
YUVAL ZOMMER

Photography by Lauren Winsor

First published in the the United States of America in 2023
by Thames & Hudson Inc., 500 Fifth Avenue, New York, New York 10110

Library of Congress Control Number 2022945671

ISBN 978-0-500-65293-0

Printed and bound in China
by Shenzhen Reliance Printing Co. Ltd.

FSC
www.fsc.org
MIX
Paper from
responsible sources
FSC® C102842

Be the first to know about our new releases,
exclusive content and author events by visiting
thamesandhudson.com
thamesandhudsonusa.com
thamesandhudson.com.au